The Night Highway

by

Christopher Hivner

First Edition: 2021
Rs. 200/-

Cyberwit.net
HIG 45 Kaushambi Kunj, Kalindipuram
Allahabad - 211011 (U.P.) India
http://www.cyberwit.net
Tel: +(91) 9415091004
E-mail: info@cyberwit.net

Printed at Repro India Limited.

Dedication

To the lonely hours of the night

Contents

Twilight

the soft glowing light from the sky when the sun is below the horizon

a period or state of obscurity, ambiguity, or gradual decline

7:09 p.m.

Searching for Everything

I'm wandering around the house
looking for inspiration.
Work is done,
it's raining outside
as twilight descends,
and I feel lost.
All rooms are quiet,
filled only with my
search for approval
from anything
I can touch.
Drawn to the window
to stare at the rain,
pulled by the impending darkness
for more instructions,
I know a night fascination
has started
while the day's meandering
has ended.
Soon I will be
behind closed doors
alone with my steady eyes
and inglorious thoughts,
soon the fascination
will extend
beyond searching for everything
to wondering whether
I deserve it.

7:35 p.m.

Escape Route

Tension
terse words
no volume
angry eyes
violating gestures

I watch the argument
from a distance,
cool evening air
rustling my shirt
as I pump gas
into my rented car.
She won't stop finger-pointing,
he can't stop the
"who cares" shrugging.
He walks away,
she follows,
there is no escape.

Tears fall
heads shake
no eye contact
turned backs
cigarettes
breathing

I don't want to stare
but am curious.
The man, tall and wiry,
paces in a jagged semi-circle,
his wife, short and wide-shouldered,
follows every step
with her own shuffle
wearing a rut in the earth.
She's talking,
can't tell if he's listening.
I put the nozzle back,
tighten the gas cap.
One last look,
he's stopped moving,
she's trying to get him to turn around.
No escape.

Physical contact attempted
by the man this time
she pulls away
no second try
he stares at the dirt

I drive away
as the couple walk
to their pick-up truck.
They climb in
without speaking,
without looking at each other.
The doors shut
enclosing them in
a metal box,
together and apart.

8:01 p.m.

Put Away Your Fancy Clothes

It's a ride
down a barren road
and the gauge is on E,
doesn't matter if you hit the brakes
you can't stop,
you won't stop.
The sun is going down,
the night can
bend your will
and snap you in half.
This life
you've chosen
bites back,
it's a ride
forward and back
until you can't
form a coherent thought
and that's when
you re-fill the gas tank,
shoot the world the finger,
pull out in front
of the Devil
and head for oblivion.

8:07 p.m.

I am the Universe

Music plays,
heavy guitar over a voice
singing in English with an accent,
the words speak
of temples
and ancient civilizations.
If I close my eyes
I am there,
chanting, swaying,
asking the emerging stars
of the sky
to lead me,
feeling the music
under my skin.
The coming night
replaces the color
in my eyes
so I can see the universe
as it is,
ageless, fearless,
holding onto its mysteries
because it doesn't want us
to comprehend.
We've ventured as far
as it will allow.
The music invades my blood
selling all that I am

to the set sun.
I am in the night
and the night is in me.
I am the universe
until tomorrow.

8:22 p.m.

Closing the Curtains

The horizon is still lit
by a crooked line of light
hugging the hill,
day holding out
for a last hurrah.
I close the curtains
as night has painted
it's latest masterpiece,
covering the houses
in the distance
with broad strokes
to hide us
from each other.

8:43 p.m.

Maybe You do Know

The sun disappears
from view
as we drive
a deserted road.
Your legs dangle
out the open side window,
your head resting
on my shoulder.
You sing along
with every song
on the radio,
your voice
a balm
to my ears
while the miles
become a blur.
I know this trip
is our swan song
but I wonder
if you do.
Always so hard to read,
you're my Faulkner novel,
ebbing and flowing
twenty-four hours
at a time.
I know I need
to move on,

the thickening blood
in my veins,
and the rain
that has just started
tell me so.
Your giggling as you scramble
to pull your legs in
and put up the window
before getting soaked
creates a smile
on my face
but doesn't
change my mind.
The wipers thumping
match my heartbeat,
the dull yellow
of the car headlights
becoming visible on the road
as daylight fades.
Still no other cars
to join us
on state road T813.
I haven't spoken a word
for twenty miles
letting you do the singing
and story telling,
but now. . .
your head is bobbing
against the seat headrest,
you gaze out the window,
swallowing either
the beading rain
or the freshly planted

corn fields
we're passing.
Maybe you do know.
This trip will be everything
or a disaster,
I don't see
an in-between.
At this moment
I just want
off this road
to nowhere
where we seem to be
the only people alive and well
with a full tank of gas.
The sky has dimmed to
an oily gray.
You turned the radio off
so the car is silent
save for the wipers
and they've become background
like the radiation
we absorb every day.
The silence of inevitability
lays over our skin,
soft silt
that dirties you up
before you notice.
I try to think
of something to say
but I'm dry.
I don't believe
you're listening anyway,
The wandering look

on your lovely face
seeks out the horizon
where long ago
meets we-have-a-future.
A stop sign appears,
an oasis
in the desert of bad thoughts.
The turn signal
fills the car with sound
and you perk up.
We turn right
onto a new two-lane road
just as darkness
clocks in for the night.

8:57 p.m.

Avalanche

I am full to bursting,
heightened arousal
and fear of everything
Charlie Brown admitted to
in his psychiatric breakthrough.
Is there a way off
this mountain?
No air to breathe,
muscles in knots,
I'm on my knees
praying for an avalanche.
Where is the hand of God
when you need a slap
in the face
to wake up?
Or a squeeze
on the shoulder
that you're not
lost in the clouds.
Base camp
do you hear me,
I can't make it back.
I'm going to watch the sunset
and wait.

9:08 p.m.

Remaining

The sweat of the day
washed down the drain,
I stand outside
to watch the sunset
and when it's gone,
when the gloaming begins,
is when the
questions start
in my head,
when my skin itches
and my heart pounds.
Soon I will be alone
in the dark,
hearing my voice
as I sob,
knowing I've gone
another day
without answers,
more hours
without you,
less of me remaining
for the future
you're not in.
The sky is still
soft blue,
barely devoid
of the sun's glamour,

a sea
for me to get lost in
while I form
tonight's queries
about my self-worth,
your disappearance
from my life,
and how they lock together.

9:32 p.m.

On a Quiet Street

The cigar tastes like
tree bark
in my mouth,
a 50 cent foible
that leaves me
spitting out slivers of leaf
after every inhalation.

Lightning bugs drift all around,
their yellow bodies blinking
on and off
like warning beacons.
I wonder about their purpose
as a cloud of smoke,
frank and biting,
layers over my head.

It's a cool night
and I should be comfortable
but I'm restless
looking for solace in nature,
too busy counting stressors
like bleating sheep
to recognize peace
on a quiet street.

The cigar is down to the nub;
I stare at the glowing end,
alive with heat,
soon to be ash,
the night sky seems darker than usual,
another firefly nods to me
in passing.
I allow the butt
to burn my fingers
while I search the silence.

9:47 p.m.

Zombies

The music played
through my headphones
while I stared out
the bus window.
Too loud drums
blared in my head
like exploding dynamite
as I waited
for the piano to push
its way to the front.
The bus made another stop
for more zombies
to get on
while a few
found freedom on the dark street.
I couldn't look
at my fellow passengers
for fear
of seeing myself.
The bus pulled away,
my reflection in the window
mumbled to me
about making amends.
I turned the music louder.
Guitars buzzing
like chainsaws
split my skull.

My reflection
gave way
to the highway
and the white line
running along the side of the road.
I am aware of movement
behind me,
an argument between zombies
over space and time,
things we never have enough of
and refuse to relinquish
an inch
of what we do own.
The line outside
blurs my vision
so all I see
is a starburst of white.
My music stops,
seconds of unbearable nothing
until the playlist shuffles
and a mournful female vocal
slips into my ears.
In the momentary void,
I heard the raised voices
of my trenchant neighbors
insisting on respect
and threatening brutality
if it isn't given.
Christ, take me to the cloud,
or your spaceship,
whatever the truth is,
get me out of here
before I sink into their swamp,

another bag of flesh
too bloated
to feel anything,
too blind
to see the world
move around me.
The bus takes a left
back into the city,
the first stop
near a liquor store.
I turn my solace louder
while the recalcitrant zombies get off
to carry their fight forward
to the land of vodka
and 50 cent wine.
On the move again
I watch the porches pass by,
the people occupying the stoops
sit motionless
like mannequins,
speaking in low voices,
selling themselves
on day break
and the fresh light it brings,
maybe one day
I can join them.
Stop after stop,
zombies get on,
zombies get off,
eyes pressed back in their heads,
hair tousled forward
as a mask,
some carry nothing,

others bundles of treasures
to hold their comfort.
When they depart the bus,
a belching dragon
that spits them out
from its sideways mouth,
they disappear into the dark,
my soundtrack forming
the only memory
I'll keep of them.
As we approach the bus depot,
the squatting beasts' lair,
the final group
prepares to depart,
shuffling to the front
against the spoken rules
of staying seated
until the dragon lands.
I let the rest of
the living dead
go ahead of me
and wait for them
to trundle off
to their place
and time wave,
Finally, it's just me
and Franklin the driver.
He watches me approach
in the rear-view mirror,
and after I drop
my coins into
the money collector,
he nods to me,

waits for me to reclaim my seat,
before we pull out
to make another round
through the night.

10:01 p.m.

Livewire

Night fell over the buildings
like oil
spilled from a rusted can.
The noises changed
from voices made of humidity and moisture
to murmurs
snaking through traffic.
A handshake
between dusk and starlight
lures me from
my hotel
to take my pulse
with tingling fingers and a breath in my throat.

10:17 p.m.

Saturday Night Poetry

Fireworks exploded in the distance
as the cigar lay between my lips,
and I listened to a baby cry from across the street.
The night air was dense,
lying on my skin like bath water.
I can't see the fireworks I can hear,
the sky holds only clouds
and the first, faint stars.
The baby has been tended to,
all is quiet on the block.
Each draw of the cigar
leaves a sweet flavor on my lips.
I see the lights of a plane
through the gathering clouds
and momentarily wish I was on it
no matter where it is going.
A barrage of firecrackers goes off,
and it feels like war has broken out.
I wonder what the baby's problem was
and was it mom or dad who was the savior.
All has gone quiet now,
I'm alone with only my thoughts,
wishing for a distraction.

10:30 p.m.

YouandI

I wanted to be with you tonight,
but that would put me in the past
when you and I
were youandI.
I wanted to be with you tonight
the way we used to,
wrapped together skin to skin
never noticing
the sun had gone down
and we had lit the candle.
I wanted tonight to be
one I would never forget
like our first together,
I even bought
the Chinese food.
Tonight, though,
is not the past.
I can't see you
no matter how hard I look,
whether in the light
or the now sweeping darkness,
the hours have gathered,
the sun is on its way
to the other side of the world
as I try to let you go.

10:50 p.m.

When the Sun Turns to Sorcery

A good opening
lays bare the ending
at least with stories
of lust and greed,
but what of wandering players
who don't know
up from sideways,
who leak into the night
one cell at a time
so they can't be seen?
Their stories
are nebulas
moving from night to day,
from standstills to searching,
part of society in the march of hours,
lost in the ether
when the Sun turns to sorcery.
The stars rotate
behind them,
the air bites,
in a bloodless affirmation
of the under being crowned
as king of velvet riches,
an empty prize,
smile and wave
to your sleeping subjects,
The opening begins

with the promise of a tale
for the saints,
until the ending
shows the truth of the night;
it is us,
minus the Sun
and its puffery,
searching for meaning
among the diamonds.

11:00 p.m.

When the Sun Goes Down

Hand-me down clothes
and a river run dry,
the tale
is in the constellations,
light through a prism
like Pink Floyd in '73.
I'll give you the details
when the sun goes down
because I can't think
in the heat.
The sky turns to
gray primer
before the black coat
is applied,
that's when the music starts
inside my head
and I can make a plan
better than yesterday's,
better than a full moon,
now I'm alive
and dancing,
now you can talk to me
before I fade away.

11:15 p.m.

Cassiopeia and a Virginia Slim

The two of us
on the porch
that night,
she's smoking a cigarette
and freezing.
I'm watching the stars
wishing I could remember
the constellations.
She says something about
not wanting to smoke anymore.
I wanted to put
my arm around her
but we weren't us anymore.
She mumbles that
she wants to go shopping
for a new coat,
I want to kiss her
but it's too late.
She doesn't like shopping,
says she never sees anything
she likes.
I shake my head
at the familiar refrain.

11:58 p.m.

There Aren't Enough Stars

Almost midnight, more light gone.

I'm outside searching the sky for which star can solve my problems, pointing to each in a childish game of eenie-meanie-miney-mo.

There aren't enough stars.

Midnight

12 o'clock at night
transition time period from one day to the next

12:07 a.m.

The Night Highway

I'm out here again,
the music of the barely there
playing on the stereo
while I drive
into a night
devoid of stars
but blinding with the artificial luminescence
of porch lights, car head lamps
and streetlights.
I am the only real thing
among the man-made
detritus of the road.

This stretch of asphalt
doesn't need me,
new tar and paint
twinkle in my high beams
as if in a stage light,
time to start our show
for another paying customer:
"Welcome to the highway lounge,
now on stage, route 462
headed for oblivion."

The darkness I drive through
is the throat of a beast
with no heart,

the center line
a consuming tongue
dragging me closer
to the belly
and the dissolving acid
of the end.
I turn the music up louder,
needing a cocoon
to hide in.
With the singer's voice
as my pulse,
the palace bones
split to the marrow
looking for the drumbeat
that counts out my mistakes
in 3/4 time.

I am real
and I am not alone
out here,
in the dim world
of the other side of the Sun.
My compatriots
pass me on the road
on the way
to their point of
absent eyes.
We don't acknowledge
each other,
just keep moving,
the hum of the car engine
a friend
in the netherworld.

There is this world
and there are others
we wish for,
there are these roads
and other paths
that would lead us
into upward grace.
There is the downtown
and there is
a fare-thee-well,
a road map
to an analgesic,
or a scrawled-on-a-napkin
line drawing
of the ever after,
ad infinitum, black death,
fuck you up
highway into the fire.

I am real
because I hear the music
and see the road,
I feel the car
underneath me.
The night highway
tries to steal my identity,
block my sight line
in the blur of
plastic and wire life
along the shoulder,
across the white line,
over the boundary
between the temperate

and the melancholy.
The night highway
feasts on me,
calls to the laity
from the church of the forlorn,
the night calls,
the road pulls,
the music charms,
I am in another place
in time
searching for veneration,
love,
understanding,
a temptation to keep me
from going back.

When the night
lays a comforting hand
on my shoulder
and we strike up
a tenuous friendship,
I go out
into the void.
I drive under the cloak,
through tunnels
of velvet darkness
on my quest
for what will make it better.
I feel like I shouldn't
exist anywhere,
not in time, space,
or the filaments
of a subatomic string.

Could the road be
my new home,
my father figure,
the everlasting concept
to my cathartic cynicism?

No.
Because the night
is temporary,
a fleeting concordance
with my search
for something,
everything, and all points
in between.
When the sun rises
you won't see me
on the highway.
You won't see me at all.

12:22 a.m.

14 Gauge

Drops of shivering light
sparkling on black silk,
the sky speaks with a tongue
fluent in dead languages,
speaks to some in mathematical equations,
to others with love and romance,
and to me without words or numbers,
but in the mystery
of the time and space
between the space and time,
the darkness
that screams void
but holds all the treasure,
winks because it knows.
The fabric pulls taut
to make the stars dance
on the wires
strung in the darkness.

12:31 a.m.

Breathing

Books sitting on shelves
like columns of soldiers,
the old man in his cushioned chair
staring out the window.
The air thickens with lingering cigar smoke
while the tobacco burns away
between his yellow fingertips.
There's nothing like a good cigar
or the first woman you ball
he once told his grandson,
too young to understand.
The boy hasn't been around, he thinks,
not remembering it's been four years.
Light from the TV that's never turned off
flickers in the evening's approaching shadows
as a young woman reveals her pain
in the silence of the muted sound.
His eyes close and sleep shrouds him.
Upstairs, the neighbor's child cries.
A muffled smack.
He turns the TV sound up.
The smell of machine oil,
a greeting from the trucks, blows through the window.
The ranks of the books are broken.
as he begins to re-read about D-Day.
But first the TV amplifies
over the din the darkness brings.

And outside, when like a jungle cat
the city's eyes open and its grin widens,
we hit the beaches in France.

1:00 a.m.

Jazz at Midnight

The road at 1 a.m.
was only a traffic light
giving out instructions
like a good soldier
even when no one was around to obey them.
He watched from the window,
a guest in his own life.
Music played a few rooms away,
the jazz that she likes.
He likes it too
if she says he should.
A car finally drives up the road
and keeps going past his house.
His hands slide back down the window
through a cloud his breath left behind.
A wailing saxophone breached his thoughts.
God, how he hated this song,
or loved it,
depending.

1:13 a.m.

There is a Thief Inside of Me

The drive goes on and on, one road becoming another in an endless parade of asphalt and sloppy line painting. The moonlight invades the car, the fullness of the space rock lighting up my face while my surroundings stay dim. The music I chose on the radio should send a charge through my veins but instead I feel dull and inert. I used to feel the wind's pins and slaps turning my face into a canvas of smooth crimson, but tonight I can only indulge a wanderlust, an urge to be somewhere else. And as soon as I reach that destination, I must leave again, to be over there. Or there. There's always another road, another turn to make. The drive goes on and on but when tomorrow comes I won't remember any of it.

1:17 a.m.

Outside

The silence laid me
on a blanket,
the darkness
folding around me
in white-light edges.
I could see through
the sky
beyond the planets
to the prayers,
a wash of connected puzzle lines
abounding with souls
walking the wire
from questions to answers.
A car passed by
to break my reverie,
standing on my porch
staring at the night sky
the stars
crashed into one another,
the beyond lost to me.
I blinked, turned,
and almost lost my balance,
walking my own wire
from alive to living.

1:31 a.m.

Night Train

The world dreamt last night
that the oceans were rising in anger,
teeth bared like a predator.
The world dreamt
of love affairs
and sexual encounters
but with everyone out of place.
When the lights went out
the world dreamt
in colors
both vibrant and muted,
of chariots
drawn by 800 horse
carrying no passengers,
only drivers
shrouded in white.
Last night,
as the tides ebbed,
sleep was purchased reluctantly
and the world dreamt
for morning to come.

2:00 a.m.

Classic Rock

I waited in the car
through the Rolling Stones,
Neil Young,
American Pie and the Beatles,
I waited through
three in a row
from The Who
and a request
for Pink Floyd,
the 17 minute one,
I waited for her
to leave his apartment,
straightening her dress,
fussing with her hair.
I waited to see it
before I hated her,
had to experience it
so I could
let go of what
I held in.
I waited until
she drove away
to shed the tears
that had been living
under my skin,
to acknowledge the sick
that was eating

my stomach.
I waited through
Cheap Trick, Zeppelin
and until
the street was empty
to get out
of my car
and walk to
the apartment
where my wife's
presence lingered
in the air
and on the bed sheets.
I hummed Ziggy Stardust
while I waited
for him
to answer the door
and sang
"Welcome to the Jungle"
as I put
a bullet in his brain.
My head
was full of static
as I walked
back to the car,
interference from somewhere
wiped my thoughts
to white.
I drove home
through weather reports,
traffic updates
and ticket give-aways,
all getting lost

in the noise
my mind
found soothing.
I waited in my driveway
through my
muttered prayer,
the neighbor's dog barking
and the
chambering of a bullet
inside my gun.
As I turned off
the car,
the DJ
put on the blues.

2:27 a.m.

The Abrasive Night

I don't have anything to say
on this enduring night,
residue of past thoughts
tie my neck
to my torso
with ropes of smoke.
If the moon
would talk to me
I'd share an anecdote or two
but the seas
are closed for the evening.
The darkness
wants to be my friend,
the silence
an acquaintance with visiting privileges.
I'm in the mood
for neither
on this unflinching night.
If I cut off a finger
I doubt I could cry out
for help
or blasphemy,
I am the picture of torpor,
down the mine
for a drink of pure finality.
I am lost
to this trenchant, striding,
overarching night.

2:57 a.m.

The Black Tar Rides the Same for Everyone

Roadside lights reached
under my chin
with slender, luminous fingers
tickling my razor-burned skin,
leading me
down the highway.
I rode the white line hard,
playing with the edge
just like she hated.
My headlights were dim,
swallowing the asphalt
in their bluish-white pyramid,
spitting it back in place
behind me
so the next guy
could drive down
the same old road.

That's the clarity,
the reveal,
we're all the same
despite the story
the lights try to tell
as you glide by
wallowing in
your private reserve,
in spite of

the road
singing Robert Johnson
in your ears
like you're the first
to ever hear it,
the black tar
rides the same
for everyone.

The lights shine
and beckon,
the yellow lines
lead you away
from the problem.
That's the rub,
those are the facts,
we're all the same.
One day,
we all
want to run.

3:14 a.m.

Morning til Night

In the wilderness
of the feral time
in our lives,
our feet slide through
the early morning dew
in a sprint
to the long day,
ferocious appetites
tearing strips of meat
from the body of the Sun,
sustenance for the
diurnal beast.

We've pushed back the
vulpine night
one more time
to reaffirm our existence
with mating calls and
lusty games of saying
the wrong thing
to the right person.
This is us,
we are we,
a marauding band
of light pirates
stealing affection from the
center of our system
to live.

The game extends,
pulling away.
We tire.
The hours creep up
buried within shadows
until we are caught
in a snare,
our ankles bitten
by the broken teeth
of the bitter dark,
our manic energy and relentless joy
nectar for
the evening clouds.
The moon laughs,
the night lifts and falls over us
like a shift,
our eyelids droop,
brains shut down.

In the wilderness
of our timidity
we give up the sun
to specters,
lay down
in the evening mist,
swallowed whole
by the midnight driver
of the lost highway.

3:37 a.m.

Absolute Zero

The void opened up
spilling restive gemstones of light
in front of me,
a checkerboard
of blue and red
telling me double stories
of which path to take.
I looked for the markers
you surely left behind
so I could follow,
but the stars put a finger
to their lips
and whispered in a hush
"Shh, we'll never tell."
Left, right, left, right,
I jumped from one blue giant
to another
searching for your perfume
or the distant echo
of your voice.
"Shh, we'll never tell,"
the stars laughed behind my back
as I changed
to the reds,
yearning for your heat,
finding only the
absolute zero

of the void.
The lush, malevolent night
opened up to me
spilling singing gemstones,
their light a siren's call
leading me away
from the mercies of
forgetting the feel
of the small of your back
and the look in your eyes
when I said your name.

3:59 a.m.

The Real Thing

There were pieces of us
in the wind
after the accident,
traces of humor,
lashes of fear,
testaments of labor,
all that made us strong,
all that shaped our legion,
heavy is the crown
for attention
from the woman
of the artful seat
and the man from
the other side.

We gathered back
forward front,
an effort to
hold our past accountable,
I believed,
you tried, failed,
there was no way out
that didn't end
with smoke
from flames
created in your eyes.

They found enough
to make a shade
of two people
that could have been us,
pale eyes staring,
lucent hands
wrapped in one another
for a show of love
while the wind
takes away the real thing.

4:15 a.m.

The Vibrating Sky

Two lane highways
lead me farther into
a night
that breaks into diamonds
twirling past
as I leak oil
in patterns on the tar
to signal
the mothership
or another ship
or any craft
to lift me away
into the black felt bosom
of the vibrating sky.
No moon tonight
for me to steer by,
no light
to reveal my craters
and dried salt seas,
the road is straight,
no snaking,
no turns into glory
or head-ons with truckers
wired by amphetamines.
The car engine whines
as I push the gas pedal
through the earth to its core,

the road's yellow lines
whip at me
like a cat o' nine tails
flaying my skin
until its striped red,
a burn for my lack of penitence,
a reminder of my past
on the chase.
A two lane road
of two way dreams
and I'm driving the wrong direction
into a night
of cut diamonds
raining down
from the vibrating sky.

4:16 a.m.

The Night has a Long Memory

The night has a long memory
and it won't
let me forget you.

4:27 a.m.

In the Dark and in the Light

The desperation found me
in the a.m.
as it always did,
lying in bed
staring through
the haze of her breathing
looking for lies
that I could live with.

My head on a pillow
of my fingers,
propped at the perfect angle
to see the wall
and it's absence
of anything of me,
mine or ours.

She turned in her sleep
slipping her arm
over my chest,
resting her head
on my shoulder
before mumbling unconsciously
about missing things.

Her hair still held remnants
of her flowery shampoo

mixed with the day's dirt.
The hairs tickled my nose
making me dream
of childhood,
my dog's fur
under my hand,
a spring sky overhead,
the horizon
showing me the way forward.

Hearing the tick of the clock
as another hour turns
I slide my hand
over her warm skin
eliciting a coo.
She pushes tighter against me
settling a soft hand
on my stomach.

In a few hours
light will return
leaving me behind
in the darkness
where I mean more to her.
The sun will steal
my relevance
leaving me nailed
to the bare wall.
The only thing of mine here
is me.

4:30 a.m.

Far Away

I matched the stars
to your eyes,
blue giants on blue pearls,
the moon
asked where you were,
far away
the only answer I had.

5:10 a.m.

Lost on the Rubicon

During the night
I can be quiet,
fleeing from sounds
on restless legs,
holding my hands
over my ears,
la la laing
into oblivion.
In the middle of the night,
I can blame someone else
and believe it to be true,
holding the delusion
until the Sun beckons morning
on my behalf
and the questioning starts anew.
When the sky is painted black,
I'm not here,
you may see me
hands held up in supplication,
lips quivering
while the prayers slide
from my mouth in a whisper
to the man on stage
but I won't see you,
not in the cotton-soft darkness
that holds me
in it arms,

not once the boundary
has been crossed,
then, I am the mist,
I am the absence of light,
I am all-knowing,
a song in every language,
a sword held to the tender throat,
a forest lost among its parts,
I am whatever
I need to be
until sunlight
re-creates me
as myself.

Dawn

the first appearance of light in the sky before sunrise
the beginning of a phenomenon or period of time

5:01 a.m.

Night's Retreat

I'm still asleep
but hear music,
the strain of violins,
slow and even,
mournful and emergent,
coat the inside of my head
with calm.
In this peace
I awaken
to the dawning day,
the sun brushing
our world
like soft cloth.
My eyes open
as the music dissipates,
I immediately
wish it to return
but the dream has evaporated
into the mist
of beginning
this morning
and that was
last night's dream,
they can't occupy
the same space
or exist as cousins
in our minds.

Night's retreat
opens the road
to the burgeoning sun
of a new day.

5:17 a.m.

The Voice of Sleep

"Wake up Frankie
and tell me a story.
     The one that doesn't end here
     where we are."

The voice emanates
from beneath my window
spiraling through pale street light
like smoke
chasing its tail.
Summer heat
pumps through my insomniac veins
while I stare
at visions of cool blue water
on my ceiling.
The fan on the floor
oscillates too slowly
to save me from melting,
while the world outside
burns to a crisp.

"Talk to me Frankie,
I can't sleep
without you telling me
     you love me."

I wait
for Frankie's voice
like every night,
dusting fairy tales to his girl
with the rhythm
of Muddy Waters,
making it not only okay,
but necessary,
to go to sleep.
Stories of
high rise buildings
draped in silk
and touching the clouds,
where the lovely people
breathe in and out,
in and out,
in and out.

"Frankie,
why are you doing this to me?
    Baby,
    you have to wake up."

5:00 a.m. and I pass each other
in the throes of drowning,
reaching a hand out
like throwing change
at a busker.
Where is the story
in the sweat of death?
Frankie's voice
is gone.
His girl won't cry,

so she begins
to sing.

I drop off to sleep
as the sun rises
over the streets.

5:22 a.m.

A New Thing

Five a.m.,
alarm blares.
I'd give anything
for two more hours
of sleep,
four if I could
steal them.
Shower, dress,
light eases
through the window.
I tried to dream
of something new
last night,
something shiny and tactile
that would slide
between my fingers,
cool to the touch.
I wanted the new thing
to show me
the sunrise,
to burn away
the residue
swallowing my skin,
the soil of the past
I climb through
every morning
that sticks to me

all day,
the new thing
was going to cleanse me,
bathe me in azure water
while angels
sang a psalm
to the heavens.

I didn't dream
last night
and now
the light is here,
daybreak,
my latest crawl
through the tunnel
of memories and missteps
spitting out dirt
and trying to breathe,
to tell myself
the day is the new thing
and this one
will be different.

5:31 a.m.

Broken

The sun rises in the sky
with or without my attention,
my dream about dad
is jumbled
confusing,
he was going to say something
and I want to go
back to sleep
but the spell is gone.
No request from me,
no desire in my heart,
the day breaks
and I am broken.

5:45 a.m.

The Engine of Everything

deep sleep dreaming
I'm alone
every strand of reality
out of my grasp

deep space dreaming
at the event horizon
my mind's here
and there

I'm lost
among the stars
I'm out here
and inside

deep sleep dreaming
everything I've ever wanted
passes by
trapped in nebula gas

I pass by
my spacesuit pure white
the engine of everything
is pure white

deep sleep dreaming
have I been taken?

I can't wake up
folded into a singularity

the universe spins
my universe is myself
and I spin
to match the engine

deep sleep dreaming
messages delivered
my understanding
still in the stars

message received
relax
when I wake
I'll take control

5:59 a.m

A Prayer at Dawn

The rain started
while I was still in bed.
No visible sunrise
this morning,
dark skies welcome me
to Thursday,
a monument
to seeing your destination
but not being able
to feel it
in the crack of your bones.
Dawn finds me
in the weeds already,
blankets over my head,
the cat meowing
for breakfast,
cement gray
seeping through the blinds
as rain pelts
the windows.
The upcoming day
looks different
from the mattress,
not as special
as it wants you to believe,
a mish-mash of hours
leading people

places they don't want to go
while their circulation slows
and body shrinks.
Let the rain come
in droplets
or in waves,
allow time
to come for me.
I won't run
or fight,
instead, I'll say
a prayer
for the dawn
to be my friend.

6:00 a.m.

Today is the Day

5:10 a.m.,
I look at the clock
to see I have 30 minutes
until my alarm goes off.
5:47 a.m.,
I have 13 minutes
until my alarm blares,
sending me a message
I don't want to hear.
5:59 a.m.,
I have one minute
to sleep,
sixty seconds
until the work day begins
and I have to
make a conscious decision.
Is this what
I really want?
Is the paycheck
every two weeks
worth it?
How do I solve
my ennui
by clocking in and out
day after day?
What are my options?
Is there . . .

beep beep beep
It's 6 a.m.,
I can sleep
for seven minutes
before the snooze alarm
goes off.

6:10 a.m.

Sunrise

he lay in his new bed
wondering what
might have been

she lay in hers
pondering the same

wishes entangled
in the strings
of the universe

they breathe in
each other's memory
tickling their lungs,
a last laugh together
before sunrise

6:14 a.m.

The Morning After Another Attempted Escape

The sun has been up
for a few minutes
but I can't
start the day.
inertia keeps
me on the porch
flicking away
one more cigarette
swearing it's my last
right before
lighting up another.
The street
is at work,
each house
producing for the economy
and the upraised spirit
of a job well done.
I called in sick
again,
although the employee handbook
doesn't mention
the disorder
of 'can't find my mojo',
that's only in
the blues songs.
I had it,

once,
but not for
more months than
I will remember.
Days are numbing,
hours dragging me along
with them
through a prosaic slog
of things I
don't care about.
The night,
a time of regeneration,
instead finds me
watching Hogan's Heroes re-runs
for hours
before I fall asleep
and dream of dreaming.
The sun's return,
the reawakening,
when all things
become new
and pure
doesn't find me in the dew
but under a blanket
looking for the sleep
I should have had
at 2 a.m.
I come outside
to feel the sun
on my face,
sensation returning
to my salty skin.
Those first moments

of the new day
feel good,
pushing resurgence
through my veins
until
that voice in my head
tells me
not to bother.
That's when I sit down
and allow the world
to move around me,
unable to participate.
The sun has been up
for a few minutes,
rising while I sink,
following its purpose
while I try to find one.
The new day
calls to me
hoping I will answer.
I wait and see.

6:29 a.m.

The Light is a Storyteller

The spark of the sun
pinches my senses
and I am awake.
The light
is a storyteller
taking the stage
for a twelve-hour play,
one long soliloquy
searching for a plot.
I feel trapped
in the audience
hearing the same story
day after day
until the curtain drops
and I have time
to wonder
where the hours have gone
and why I didn't
harvest the pearls
when I had a chance.

6:40 a.m.

Tick Tock

Time coded syncopations,
my heart restarts
on the first breath
of morning air
jolted by rebirth.
My nightly death,
charged to the
even hours
of dark contemplation
has been subverted
once more
by the odd hours
of fascination
of what comes next
and the hope
that it's all
worth it.

6:48 a.m.

The Nebula of Before and After

I haven't been here
in a while,
this place,
this nebula of
before and after
where I usually live.
Been trying something different,
staying home,
walking slow steps,
hearing only today's calls
and affirmations
that glide on the slipstream
of my shaken confidence.
The other place,
other space,
pulls me in
like an addiction,
what if . . .
why did . . .
if I could go back . . .
The cloud is intoxicating,
infuriating,
maddening,
an ever present
screaming-in-my-face
coffee-breathed dragon
that sets me alight

each morning
before my eyes even open.
I'm here now
in my new clothes
facing another test,
true or false,
check one.
I hope the teacher
grades on a curve.

7:01 a.m.

Old Blood

When the sun
comes over the trees
I know
another day has begun
without you.
A small arc
of light
begins my journey
from morning
through night
remembering
all the moments
I'd like to forget
if only my mind
didn't hate me.
It is lyrical
the way your voice
lilts through my ears
even though
I haven't heard you speak
since the day
we crumbled
like an ancient monolith
shaken by the earth.
I wish the sun
would stay
where it belongs

after night
takes over,
let me alone
with its new day fervor,
allow me to sleep
all day
until I pass you
through my system,
old blood for new,
back off
yellow demon
and let me breathe,
it's only been
ten thousand days.
When the sun
comes over the trees
I have to wake up.

7:17 a.m.

I Rise in the Sky

I made the left turn
just like the fortune cookie told me to,
down a dirt lane,
specks of mottled white
staring from the roadside darkness
at the interloper.
I drove through the night,
my inconsistent will
holding me to the sun
as it rose in the sky.

I walked through the door
just like the fortune teller told me to,
and she was there,
opaque and languorous,
dressed in white lace,
staring at nothing
while fireworks ignited around her,
the moon a bauble against her ear
as it rose in the sky.

I ran with scissors under a ladder,
just like the old Gypsy told me to,
defying the universe,
spurning good sense
to live in sin with ignorance.
I felt alive for a few seconds

before the burning in my chest
slowed me, dropped me, left me for dead,
the north star shining in my eyes
as it rose in the sky.

I took the advice
of anyone with an opinion,
wandered their path,
spoke their words,
to the detriment of all things
until I got in my car
and drove away
from lovers and friends,
enemies and unknowns,
to find my double helix,
the mist that contains me
as I rise in the sky.

7:57 a.m.

Unfolded

I am in the sky
floating upward to God

I am in the clouds,
cumulonimbus over Philadelphia

I am unaware of anything
except freedom

I am flying with the birds
and they revere me

I am elusive and migratory,
illusory and sacrificial

I am unleashed

I am dangerous

I am

Acknowledgments

"On a Quiet Street" was originally published in *Driftwood Bay* in 2012

"Livewire" was originally published in *The Blue Hour* in 2013

"Saturday Night Poetry" was originally published in *Wax* in 2018

"When the Sun Turns to Sorcery" was originally published in *Yellow Mama* in 2021

"When the Sun Goes Down" was originally published in *Culture Cult* in 2018

"Cassiopeia and a Virginia Slim" was originally published in *Dead Snakes* in 2016

"14 Gauge" was originally published in *Culture Cult* in 2018

"Breathing" was originally published in the *Edged in Blue* chapbook in 2004

"Outside" was originally published in *Dead Snakes* in 2016

"Night Train" was originally published in *Underground Voices* in 2010

"Classic Rock" was originally published in *Dead Snakes* in 2012

"The Abrasive Night" was originally published in *Record Magazine* in 2018

"The Black Tar Rides the Same for Everyone" was originally published in *Dead Snakes* in 2012

"The Real Thing" was originally published in *Erothanatos* in 2019

"The Vibrating Sky" was originally published in *Anti-Heroin Chic* in 2017

"In the Dark and In the Light" was originally published in *Dead Snakes* in 2013

"Far Away" was originally published in *Dead Snakes* in 2015

"The Voice of Sleep" was originally published in *Five* in 2015

"The Engine of Everything" was originally published in the *Secrets and Dreams* anthology in 2015

"Unfolded" was originally published in *Syzygy* in 2015